How Does She Do It? Who Does She Think She Is?

Onedia N. Gage, Ph.D., CLC

The Secrets
of My
Success

Personal & Business Coaching

How Does She Do It?

Who Does She Think She Is?

The Secrets of My Success

Personal & Business Coaching

How Does She Do It?

Who Does She Think She Is?

ONEDIA NICOLE GAGE, PH. D., CLC

How Does She Do It? Who Does She Think She Is?

DEDICATION

This is for you, if . . .

You can't seem to get past step two

You can't seem to close the deal

You can't seem to lift your head away from your chest

You can't figure out why you can't be successful

You don't have any support for your dreams

This is for you.

Please keep your focus!

Library of Congress

The Secrets of My Success

Personal & Business Coaching

How Does She Do It? Who Does She Think She Is?

Purple Ink, Inc. Press

For Information address:
Purple Ink, Inc.
1202 E. 1st St., 14931,
Humble, TX 77347
www.purpleink.net ♦ onediagage@purpleink.net

Onedia Gage Speaks

www.onediagagespeaks.com ♦
onediagage@onediagagespeaks.com

ISBN:

978-1-939119-82-7

Printed in the United States

SCRIPTURES

The Gage Remix of my favorite scriptures.

Fearfully and wonderfully made.

Psalms 139:14

More than a conqueror.

Romans 8

Extravagance.

1 Corinthians 13:13b

Without faith it is impossible to please God.

Hebrews 11:6

Love: how wide and long and high and deep is the love of Christ.

Ephesians 3:14-21

Other Books by

Onedia N. Gage, Ph. D., CLC

Are You Ready for 9th Grade . . . Again? A Family's Guide to Success
As We Grow Together Daily Devotional for Expectant Couples
As We Grow Together Prayer Journal for Expectant Couples
As We Grow Together Bible Study: Her Workbook
As We Grow Together Bible Study: His Workbook
Because I Do: A Working Marriage—Her Workbook
Because I Do: A Working Marriage—His Workbook
The Best 40 Days of My Life: A Journey of Spiritual Renewal
The Blue Print: Poetry for the Soul
From Fat to Fit in 90 Days: A Fitness Journal
From Two to One: The Notebook for the Christian Couple
Hannah's Voice: Powerful Lessons in Prayer
The Heart of a Woman: The Depth of Her Soul
Her Story The Legacy of Her Fight: The Bible Study
Her Story The Legacy of Her Fight: The Devotional
Her Story The Legacy of Her Fight: The Legacy Journal
Her Story The Legacy of Her Fight: Prayers and Journal
I Am.: 90 Days of Powerful Words: Affirmation and Advice for Girls
ily! A Mother-Daughter Relationship Workbook
In 90 Days: What Will You Do?
In Her Own Words: Notebook for the Christian Woman
In Purple Ink: Poetry for the Spirit
In Your Hands: A Dad's Impact on His Daughter's Self-Esteem
Intensive Couples Retreat: Her Workbook
Intensive Couples Retreat: His Workbook
Living A Whole Life: Sermons Which Prompt, Provoke, and Provide
Life
Living An Authentic Life
Love Letters to God from a Teenage Girl
The Measure of a Woman: The Details of Her Soul
The Notebook: For Me, About Me, By Me
The Notebook for the Christian Teen
On the Same Team
On This Journey Daily Devotional for Young People
On This Journey Prayer Journal for Young People
On This Journey Prayer Journal for Young People, Vol. 2

One Day More Than We Deserve Prayer Journal for the Growing Christian

Promises, Promises: A Christian Novel

Queen in the Making: 30-Week Bible Study for Teen Girls

Queen in the Making: 30 Week Bible Study for Teen Girls Leader's Guide

The Secrets of My Success: Business Coaching How does she do it? Who does she think she is?

Serve the Staff: The Impact of a Healthy Social-Emotional Climate and Culture

She Spoke Volumes . . . And Then Some

Six Months of Solitude: The Sanctity of Singleness Notebook

Six Months of Solitude: The Sanctity of Singleness Prayers and Journal

There's a Queen Within: Her Journey to Building Self—Worth

Tools for These Times: Timely Sermons for Uncertain Times

The Vision Notebook

Walking Tall with a Broken Life

What Did You Say?: Affirmations. Encouragement. Motivation.

With a Crown and No Home

With An Anointed Voice: The Power of Prayer

A Woman Like Me: A Bible Study for Women to Survive Our Times

A Woman Like Me: A Daily Devotional for Women to Survive Our Times

A Woman Like Me (a sermonic study): Lessons for Us Women

Yielded and Submitted: A Woman's Journey for a Life Dedicated to God

Yielded and Submitted: A Woman's Journey for a Life Dedicated to God An Intimate Study

Yielded and Submitted: A Woman's Journey for a Life Dedicated to God Prayers and Journal

The Nehemiah Character Series

Nehemiah and His Basketball
Nehemiah and His Big Sister
Nehemiah and His Bike
Nehemiah and His Flag Football Team
Nehemiah and His Football
Nehemiah and His Golf Clubs
Nehemiah and Math

Nehemiah and the Bully
Nehemiah and the Busy Day
Nehemiah and the Class Field Trip
Nehemiah and the Substitute for the Substitute
Nehemiah Can Swim
Nehemiah Found the Mud
Nehemiah Reads to Mommy
Nehemiah Writes Just Like Mommy
Nehemiah, the Hot Dog, and the Broccoli
Nehemiah's Family Vacation
Nehemiah's Favorite Teacher Returns to School
Nehemiah's First Day of School
Nehemiah's Sister Moved
Nehemiah's Visit to the Hospital

TABLE OF CONTENTS

How Does She Do It? Who Does She Think She Is?

18

Introduction

The Secrets of My Success: Personal and Business Coaching. 'How does she do it' is a popular question. People look at me and wonder how I do everything that I do. They asked that question because they compare their life to mine. They are considering what they wanted to do by a certain age. If they have not accomplished 'that' then they wonder why other people have achieved 'that'.

It is unbelievable the Personal Achievement that I have accomplished in my lifetime. It is quite a feat. I have not achieved all that I set out to do, but I have also achieved things I never dreamed of. I know that my life is nothing short of amazing. I hope that it continues for the balance of my life.

The secrets that I will share will not be profound or dramatic. The concepts are quite simple but the way you engage those characteristics is the Difference Maker – it is how you achieve the amazing results that you desire. I have been a doer all of my life. I risk image and pride, ego and character, in order to overcome the odds which seem to be positioned before me.

For me, when I don't achieve my goal, it is because I am not putting enough energy toward the project or activity. When I learned that about myself, I was startled. It was an eye-opening moment. I will never ask myself again "what was wrong with me" because that meant that I needed to address my motivation about the matter.

As I address the questions and the details of my journey, I want to ensure that you understand that the first step to achievement is to realize your competition is yourself and only yourself.

Let's get ready for the journey and the work in which you will engage so that you can reach your goals.

The Secrets of My Success!

My Life's Story

I grew up in humble beginnings. I did not have money. I was not privileged as defined by societal measures. I had difficulty in making friends because I didn't live close to the school where I attended and there were social organizations to which I did not belong. My fellow classmates also lived close to each other and they visited each other often. I am not a first-generation college graduate. I don't have a tragic story to share or to compel others with, however my story is impactful.

A broken home? Yes. Divorced and a survivor of my own divorce. During that time, I produced the best and the most work that I've ever produced. I had a different motivation: I had to defy the statistics built against me. Kids of divorce parents are considered to be disengaged because they are distracted and emotionally taxed. No one expects anything from those children. I needed to ensure that I did not become that child that everyone excuses and no one expects anything from. I had to break the norm and the cycle.

There is a high rate of depression for women who are divorced. I did not want that to define me or the balance of my life. Before I divorced, I had resumed pursuing my goals that had been abandoned in order to be a good wife and a great mother. As I saw the end of that union coming, I decided to take charge of my life and my new journey.

I was committed to my success for two reasons. I wanted the world to see that I was not broken. I also needed my children to see that I was more than their father told him about me. I needed them to see an overcomer, and survivor that breaks down the odds that are real and the ones which are assumed. I graduated with my undergraduate degree after two years of not attending college in the second summer sessions, after a breakup, before I met my ex-husband. I completed 18 hours in one summer session. After major terrible events, I accomplish great things. I published my first book in 2000; my second one was published in 2001. It was 7 years later when I published books three and four. There are years when I publish multiple books and others when I publish nothing.

I do not honor the concept of pacing myself. I do not consider the idea of overachievement. Based on the circulation of over 100 ISBN numbers, I feel like I still have work to do. I still have a list of books to write and activities to complete. This one is included in that list. My life has been challenging but not in a cumbersome way. I have not experienced nearly the tragedies that other people have experienced, and for that I am extremely grateful.

I want to be a good steward on my talents and gifts as well. The best way to be grateful for what you are gifted with is to use them and then they will benefit others.

When I understood that my life was valuable so that I could serve others and also help them to be great. Because of that, I will not stop helping others.

As far as my life is concerned, it is fixed. I seem to be in the places where I can serve best. Sometimes I am in agreement, then there are other times when I am in total disagreement about where I am being asked to serve.

I can account for my efforts and my actions even though I cannot guarantee my results. I cannot say enough times that I have battled most of the events in my life alone, only with the support of my children. My family has been absent for quite a bit of my milestones, choosing to be absent at crucial moments. Still, I have to persist. I have to move forward.

My great-grandparents and my father passed away before I was really successful. They would be proud of where I am right now. They were my biggest supporters for my whole life.

If you're ready for the real information and the real work, let's get started!

The Goal List

I have had a goal list since I was a teenager. Please understand that you may have a list but if that list does not have any dates on it then this is a wish list or a nice to have/do list. You need to put a date to accomplish by on that page this date urges accomplishment. You need a deadline so that you are actively working towards the goal. In order to achieve the goal that you have set, you need to consider your lifestyle as you decide when you can achieve that goal. You need to be aggressively realistic in pursuit of your goals.

Your goals on extension and an expression of who you are. Your goals are representative of your personality. Your goal should be precise and specific. You need to share your goals with others so that you are accountable for achieving your goals.

The mistake that most people make is that they don't have an accountability partner. They tried to pursue the goals in silo, in secrecy. That is not enough in order to obtain the goal. Achieving some of your goals requires time and energy, Imagination and innovation.

Your creativity is also required. rank the goals in order of importance and then of difficulty. This ranking will help you prioritize in which order that you need to pursue the goals.

It may be wise to only pursue one or two goals at a time. The focus at each requires will be time consuming. you don't want to lose focus or motivation. Also, you don't want to get so caught up with the list that the goal does not become attained. The goal list is not to be obsessed with or over. The goal list is a guide, not the total authority over your life.

The goal will enhance and possibly redefine you as a person. your goals will identify you. Once you start to pursue your goals, you should feel different about yourself.

Planning is critical to the success of your goals. Time management is the companion to the planning element.

Revise the goal list each year. you will add. You may even subtract. The purpose is to reevaluate your mission statement, vision statement, and values. If your goals do not align with those elements, then you need to revise the goal list.

Focus on the end result. Focus on the joy of the pursuit. Focus on the lessons that you have learned. Focus on the elements that you can share with others. Focus on how your work ethic will be repeated through the lives of your children and family, along with others which you influence.

Write the goals out: the boldest and the absolute scariest.

Vision and Vision Boarding

The vision of your life is the culmination of your desires, talents, skills, and future.

Vision is hard to write initially and even harder to embrace. Some people have difficulty distinguishing between the two elements: the mission and the vision.

In 2000, there was a wave of vision boarding which entailed using magazines and other resources to post pictures of your dreams and desires on a poster so you can see it daily and it was posted in full view so that it is not forgotten or swept under the proverbial rug.

Vision requires focus. Your vision will determine your growth and your future. Vision will be the determination of the success you achieve.

My vision for myself and my companies and activities is driven by my desire to achieve my goals and to be an example for my children and those people that I mentor and coach. My vision is aggressive. It is overwhelming. It is scary. It is outrageous. It is outlandish. It is offensive. My vision is so big that others stand around and watch. My vision is almost impossible. However, I keep making the vision of reality.

A vision statement is defined as a written declaration clarifying your business's meaning and purpose for stakeholders, especially those most impacting of and the most impacted.

My vision is audacious! Why is it so over the top? I want to make the fullness of my business and my life. I want to achieve so much because of my talents and my dreams. Those are two different lists and because of the extensiveness of those two lists when they are merged, the result was the vision and all that it entails.

This vision is a start and the progress of the greatness of the results. This is the birth of excellence, that is the goal of all achievement. The vision board is a reminder that we have a job and a destination: this journey. This journey leads to some, several, destinations. These destinations produce results.

Vision board is both verbal, visual, and written. It is easy to access as a reference. The ability to reference the vision is necessary so that you can achieve the items on the board or list. The vision for your life needs to remain alive at all times. In order to make that vision come alive, it needs to be visible and viewed and reviewed at a minimum every other day. That review will then require you to make plans and create a space for that accomplishment. As you develop those plans and carry out those plans to achieve those goals, you will face some obstacles, some pain, however it is more important to attempt the goal rather than to keep looking at the list or to keep thinking about the list.

Vision items need a date so that you do not think that it is a suggestion. It is important that you achieve something on a regular basis so that you remain motivated. This motivation is critical so that you do not quit. Quitting will stall or delay or completely derail your vision. If you take a break while pursuing another item, then you will still be making progress.

How do you develop that list of goals? It is the thing that you would do for free and that keeps you up at night. You cannot stop talking about or thinking about. It is what you dream about and sketch about. It is what you look at often and Google regularly. These goals which become part of your vision are what should consume your time. If your goals are not the focus of the result of that time, then you need to redirect that time. The time that you spend on what is important is what you will achieve. Vision is a journey, rather than a destination.

Vision boarding helps you to realize your journey in a more efficient manner.

Dreams

I believe that I have been dreaming since I arrived on this earth. I can dream in such a manner the others went and cringe, hide and reconsider their lives. My dreams are so big and outlandish that they are offensive. In the span of eighteen months, I had published my first book, got a promotion, got married, expected my first child, built my first home, and was in the midst of publishing my second book when I heard two different comments. The first one was 'how do you top the achievements of the last eighteen months.' The second one was 'I thought you had so much going on that you would have forgotten about that next book.'

The first statement shared some clarity on the life that I had sought to lead. I was a climber: I always looked up, not often looking around, and certainly not looking back. When I consider my life, I consider the toil and snare to be the motivational factors of the whole achievement mantra. I cannot think of a time when I was not trying to accomplish something.

The dream was a thought. The dream was a simple muse. Then one day you decide that you want that dream to be your reality. That thought causes the work to start, then the dream is closer to a reality. The dream does not work until you do. I do not own the credit for that statement, but I have proof that it is true.

I have a two-page list of dreams. In 2007, I was disappointed in myself for not finishing my educational pursuit for my masters of business administration. My marriage was failing and flailing, so I dusted off my dream list and started to pick up the lowest hanging fruit. The first item was that MBA degree. Next was the master's degree in education. I graduated with two degrees and 3 years. I finished several books. I started my publishing firm. This move sent a message to everyone around me that dreams are only a reality when followed by actions. I took a lot of actions. These persistent and fierce actions led to some great results as well as some powerful learnings. I answered a question as well: I topped 2000 and 2001 with 2009 and 2010. Then I did it again. And again. And again.

In 2014, I realized that I had just been an achievement machine. I had been working so much that I published my 20th book. Whew! I did not include the ebooks. This was an average of more than one book per year. As of 2024, I have authored more than 78 books. That is an average of 3.25 books per year over 24 years. That was not the original goal or dream. I just intended to publish and author two books total! 78 books later, and I am still amazed. I am still excited. I am still overwhelmed. I am still in awe. I am still blessed. I am still researching. I am still sharing. I am still championing the world around me. I am still keeping my word about my intention to impact others with my knowledge. I do not lose anything by sharing my knowledge. My selflessness does not put me at a disadvantage or loss.

Dreams require work. Because I want my dreams to be a reality, then I commit my time to my dreams. I don't watch much television. I don't waste a lot of time. I don't engage in activities which are not designed to achieve my dreams.

When you consider travel, television, or time for your dreams, what will the decision-making criteria be? What will you spend your time doing? Your decision will make the difference between achievement and thinking about the dream(s) years later. If you are only thinking about them, then there's a 100% chance that they will never become a reality.

How important are those dreams to you? If you are satisfied with just thinking about them, then do nothing. But if you are awake at night because you have not reached the goal or achieved the dream, then some work may need to be in the forecast.

Learning and Reading

If the lifelong learner definition needed a photograph, then it would probably be mine which is listed. I have loved to read since I knew how to read. My mother's budget had to include buying books for me regardless if she wanted to or if she actually could afford it or not.

Reading is how you discover the secrets of all things. There's a statement that states if you want to keep anything a secret then put it between the covers of a book. I am on a quest for all of the secrets. In order to continue to learn, then you need to read and seek knowledge. In this technological generation, there is a tendency to bypass reading substantive material for Wikipedia and other similar sources. This is not enough to be considered learning and to have gained actual knowledge.

Reading actual research based information as well as reputable sources along with field experts who have chosen to publish is how learning takes place.

Reading is time consuming. Audio books have been devised to assist with that however, those books do not always have the complete content of the original book. Upon realizing that caveat, I then decided that the shortcut was not quite worth the missing information. For that reason, I would rather read the entire document personally.

I verify what I hear from various sources. I do not concern myself about the validity of the source. I still verify. This verification is how I determine how I respect that person going forward.

Reading also shapes your character, builds your work ethic, and perseverance. Reading keeps you informed. Without reading, you will forever depend on the world of others to share with you what is going on. They may lie to you because you are known not to verify the information that you are given.

I attempt to share reading with everyone because it is the most critical method to obtain information. Learning is critical for growth. I learn by reading. listening and writing. How do you learn? When was the last time you read a book? Or magazine? Or something that was not on the internet?

Teaching/Giving

"I don't lose anything by sharing what I know."

Dr. Onedia Gage

I realized that teaching is a gift. And that I do it all the time. In order to teach, I also need knowledge so I am a lifelong learner. I want others to learn. No one can steal, discount, discredit, or discriminate against your knowledge. Young people often reject knowledge and education. As an adult, you have learned to appreciate where your education has taken you. And what that education has afforded you. You cannot say that you regret learning what you know.

It is amazing how your previously experienced knowledge comes to you right in time for the exact situation where you need it.

"Intuition does not come to the unprepared mind."

Dr. Onedia Gage

Teaching is tiring and rewarding, selfless and reflective. You can only teach what you know, based on learning and experience.

Teaching benefits me as much as it benefits the students whom I serve. I find myself teaching all of the time. The most rewarding part of my work is teaching my biological children what I wish that I knew at their age. I am trying to teach them such that they benefit from my experiences. And my mistakes.

Teaching reminds me of what I don't know and what I need and want to know. Teaching facilitates growth. The teacher learns and the audience grows as well. The teacher usually studies and prepares for each lesson or presentation.

I teach because I was gifted and called to share. If I don't use my gifts properly, I will lose these gifts. Teaching is sharing. and equipping. and helping others to form independence. This is not your average exchange. Teaching assures a palatable or fertile ground. Learning initiates trust. I teach and give of myself because I wish to be the blessing that no one was to me. I say that and people around me get nervous.

No one can imagine that I have achieved what I have without a solid support system. I promise that I would do better than I experienced. I decided I would invest in others differently. I essentially trained and taught people how to be great but I do not announce my goal outcomes.

As a previous retail manager, I trained many people. My leadership reputation was based on my employees' abilities and my store's performance numbers. But the ultimate report card is when the employee shares their a-ha moments. The second is when the doubt of others is resolved. I was working and one of my former employees was home for the holidays and came by to visit. He asked to transfer to the store near his college. I agreed and facilitated the process. I asked how it was going; however, I did not know that the visit was intentional. He answered me by saying that he has spent most of his 8-hour shifts in the fitting room. I was thinking 'boring.' But he continues with 'I want to thank you.' 'For?' I asked. 'I cannot have imagined that I was more ready than I could ever imagine.' 'What do you mean?' He goes on to share that one of the managers asked about being cashier trained. "Yes," he replied. They were surprised. They asked about the sales floor. He said yes; they were again surprised. They then asked about roll out (new floor sets). Then I got offended,' he said. "They seemed to not understand why I knew so much so I asked. They said that 'you are so well cross trained. Most people don't know what you know. Most managers don't usually train all associates at this level. I was then surprised and more so astonished that I had misjudged and misunderstood you. I want to apologize and to thank you. You never kept anything from us. You are selfless about your knowledge. You prepared us to be effective everywhere. We didn't even know. I truly apologize for not getting it while I was here. I want to thank you for believing in us. I didn't appreciate you like I should have."

"Thank you for sharing this with me. I don't have any idea why other managers do not feel the need to train their teams. We are too small to compartmentalize people. I needed you to be versatile to help the building to move forward and make progress. I am glad that you were able to become a valuable member to that team. I am definitely different from my colleagues. I train the team because I trust the team. I built the team in order to be successful. I don't lose, but gain it all, when I teach you what I know. Good luck with everything. I am glad that you learned who I am." I am still overwhelmed by about his experience.

Kelly came into the building for a part-time job and I hired her. I then trained her to cover the men's department because I lacked an assistant manager. She rose to the assignment, serving flawlessly. She soaked up my directions and advice and my anecdotes so that she could be successful. After six intense weeks, Kelly was the newest assistant manager in the building. She worked hard.

She learned how to read the reports related to sales and growth patterns. She learned a lot. She made a lot of progress. She was successful. She amazed herself. We were moving along with great progress. One afternoon, Kelly entered my office in tears. I could not understand her while she was trying to speak but the tears overtook her words. After she calmed down, she revealed that her husband was being transferred back to College Station, Texas. She was upset because she did not know what it meant for her new career.

After I settled her down, I made two phone calls. The first was to my district manager so that I could ask her about the possibilities. The second call was because of the first. As a result of the first call, I called the store manager in College Station because he had an associate manager position available. He expressed that he did not want to feel forced to accept her. She was an assistant manager. Through the process and the policies, Kelly was transferred. All was well.

The annual managers meeting was in Orlando, Florida that year. All of the Houston and surrounding area managers were eating together. In the line of conversation, my name was said. Then the funniest question ever happened: "Onedia? Where is she? I need to talk to her."

My Houston colleagues were immediately silent. I broke the silence and said, "Yes, that's me and you are?"

He then said, "Thank you. I want to thank you. I want to apologize that I did not trust you. Kelly is indeed amazing. We just promoted her to associate manager."

He was still talking when I stopped listening because I mentally revisited her first day we met. She was just looking for a part-time job so that she could have something to do while her husband was at work. My giving changes lives even when I am not present.

I was so proud of her tenure and intentional intensity which led to her being in a great place. I was proud to be her mentor, leader, and her advocate.

It did not and does not cost me anything to share my knowledge with others.

Teaching and giving of myself to others has been key to my success and to the success of those who I mentor.

Planning

I plan. I plan. I plan.

In October of each year, I sit down and plan my next year. This planning session is designed to help me prepare and to be prepared. I have always kept a calendar. I write everything down; not only because I don't want to forget something, but also so that I don't miss anything. The other piece is that I have a journal of where I have been and what I have achieved. Planning means that your goals are priority.

Planning means that you have taken the time to be intentional about your time. My time needs to be accounted for. I do not waste time. I am not a procrastinator. I am not an over-analyzer. I like to take action.

Planning provides a pathway for achieving the goals which I set. Planning also ensures that I have all of the materials that I need. Planning means that I don't neglect any of my priorities. Planning does not negate spontaneity but the spontaneity has an opportunity to take place because that is needed. There is no need to not have fun or do something off script just because it is not on the initial calendar.

Planning also shows me where I need to add events and activities. Planning assists me with my focus.

Focus

"Your focus needs much more focus." Jordan Broussard

Focus begets discipline. Focus is the path to achievement. Focus is not taking your attention off of a particular subject.

I have incredible focus. I do not 'talk' about it. I do 'it'. My focus is a gift and I protect it with all that I am. I drive my life through achievement by the path of focus.

Why do people have issues with focus? I am not sure. There are so many labels for medical issues which stop focus. I do not give any of them attention in my life. I have learned that I may have an undiagnosed case of ADHD or ADD. These are defined as attention deficit hyperactivity disorder and attention deficit disorder. Whether I have those or not does not matter; what matters is that I use those issues to do more than my counterparts. If I can achieve more because I can multitask and I can operate off of a list of goals and desires, then maybe use my methods rather than the ones which keep you from achieving your goals.

One of my mantras is: "follow your own advice." When I give advice, I follow it first - that is how it became advice.

I can only imagine what other people think when we discuss what I have achieved. I still am working on those items which I believe are a part of my purpose and calling.

Focus is also about making choices. I try to travel as much as possible. I do not watch much television. I don't go out much either. I do not consider any of that wasting time. I do consider some of that time that I can reroute to my goal list. I do not need to watch that show in real time. I can watch it after I finish the current project.

Focus is discipline in action. Focus also means that you are not deterred by the discouraging words of others. You may want to consider some distance from people around you may say that you don't need to do that or they thought you would have forgotten about it or changed your mind and course. Any words or deeds which cause you to doubt or change the course of the path you should be taking as not in your favor. Focus is not quitting. Some things do not happen when you have them planned but at a different time when it should happen. This one is hard for me. I want everything accomplished now, so I work now.

May your focus develop more focus.

Perseverance

I should have quit every day, every week, every month, and every year and every decade. I should have given up on every aspect of my life. Yet I keep at it - whatever it is. I keep trying. The odds are always against me. Yet, I keep defying the very odds presented to me.

What have I made it through? Divorce. Inconsistant parents. Inconsistant family. Homelessness. Lack of love. Poor credit. Failed relationships. Repossessions. Those are events and situations, however they are not enough to stop me. I hope no one else is stopped by these circumstances either.

I thought about suicide one time. I told my mother. I was probably 12. She said that's not a thing; go back to your room. We need to learn how to identify the pain and events which actually caused you to stretch and grow. These events help us to build a capacity for perseverance: A don't quit–can't quit attitude.

I can't afford to quit or even waiver a little bit; the calling on my life can't afford that. This is not what leaders, or winners do. Those events and situations caused me to look at life differently. They made me stop and reevaluate my methods and my mechanisms. People do not follow, respect, or invest in quitters.

I have endured my life. I have managed to get past the toughest of times as I define tough. I keep pressing toward my goals because I want to see the outcome of my efforts. Others are already counting me out and attempting to disqualify me, so I can't let them be right. My enemies cannot win by trying to keep me in fear of their opinion. My perseverance gives others hope and the ability to do the same.

The Question of Should I Quit

Just because I did not quit does not mean that I did not consider the concept. People only think of quitting as starting and not finishing. That is not the only version of quitting. It is actually not the majority.

The majority of quitting happens because of dreams which are never pursued and projects which were never started. This is because of doubt, lack of financial resources, and lack of encouragement and support. The doubt - can I actually do it? - is real and it dominates the minds and the hearts of many. I do not have the actual statistics on what is not achieved because of the lack of resources, but I know for sure that it is real.

Once the courage is established, then the financial resources may be the next obstacle to overcome. What is required to create, market, sell, and distribute your project/widget?

Then there is the emotional support which is needed in order to sustain the motivation and energy to continue the work to which we are assigned to pursue.

I had published my first book. After that I got married, started building a home, and got pregnant, I was about to publish my second book. There were two things which were said to me that made me consider what stalls others from pursuing their goals and dreams. The first statement was how do you top that segment of accomplishments. The second one was I thought you would have forgotten about that, referring to the next book that I was about to publish.

Neither of them was encouragement to continue impacting or inspiring or even achieving. They had two different perspectives of the same events. A person other than me may have been influenced to do nothing. They might try to shrink back into the background. They may feel bad about doing more than others for achievement. I didn't do that. I stepped out and did it over and over and over again.

Quitting includes every action that is required to achieve greatness.

At the time, you have considered quitting, could you have spent that time on other solutions? I have wanted to quit, but did not. I redirected my energy to push in another direction so that I could still reach my achievement and deadline.

If you quit, will you ever be able to restart this or any other project?

Is there no other recourse?

Have you exhausted all of the possibilities?

Are there resources that you need but cannot access?

Are there people that you need but have not called?

Is this hard or impossible?

What will happen if you quit but someone else achieves the goal and completes the project?

I quit something once and I did not consider all the consequences, so my children suffered. I have not quit anything since then without understanding the full range of the outcomes and possibilities. I have left places of employment because of the lack of leadership in the culture and climate of the organization. That was not me quitting my cause, purpose, or calling. At that point, it was closure for the reason why I was there.

If you are pursuing your life's work, but you stop then that is quitting. What could possibly cause you to quit? If you are purposed, then you don't quit. You can change the way you pursue that purpose, but you don't quit.

Mission Statement

I live by a mission statement. A mission statement is the description of a company's culture, value, or purpose for being. A mission statement is defined as an action-based statement that declares the purpose of an organization and how they serve their customers.

I live by a mission statement which states that I will assist and promote the upliftment of girls and women in order to increase their self-esteem. As women and girls enhance their self-esteem, they also increase accomplishments and achievements in all areas of their lives.

This is what I live to do: increase the self-esteem of other females. everything I do leads to this one goal, this one task, this one outcome.

Mission statements require that the entity remains focused and steadfast. This means that companies stay focused on the central goal and not anything extra or off course.

Mission statements ensure that the company accomplished the goals because distractions are avoided. Imagine what cannot be achieved because you cannot stay focused on the tasks at hand. When reflect on why you're not achieving any of your goals, is it because you cannot keep focused or stay grounded in the work?

Mission statements require edits and revisions. Further, mission statements require work in order to fine-tune and sharpen the statement. This is essential to the work.

If there is work to do, then there should be a mission statement.

Each year, I review the statement and revise as needed. This review grounds the work for the future. This compels the work forward. The mission statement is the mechanism by which the work is done.

Vision Statement

The vision statement is what I do, how I do it, and why I do it. My vision statement reveals my focus. I write books with the intention of enhancing the self-esteem of any girl and woman.

My vision statement propels me forward, requires that I do not procrastinate, and that I complete my projects and tasks.

I impact the lives of others daily so when I don't complete my projects, goals, tasks or mission, then I may fail someone who is desperately praying and hoping that I use my gifts and talents to save them from themselves. I am put here to help her to lift her chin away from her chest so that she can see her future and work to sustain her future so that she can see her own success.

My vision has saved the lives of many in various ways. There are people whom I have changed the nature of their lives by simply living my purpose and remaining committed to my vision, mission and purpose.

Vision is essential to success.

Values

What do I hold true and cherish? What means the most to me? What do I need to be a contributor to society?

What I spend my time on is what I value. The value of time spent is how I decide the level of importance.

We do many things - events, trips, stuff - but how do we decide what is more important than something else. Some things are obvious; others are more subtle.

Values are what matters over everything. I make choices based on those values. I say no because of those values. I change the path we take because of the decisions which are driven by values.

Values ensure that your integrity remains intact. Values are lost in desperation or hopelessness or fear. My values must remain steadfast - I cannot waiver. I cannot quit. I cannot get off course because people that I do not know are counting on me to do something that is outstanding and courageous, amazing and audacious because she needs hope in her life because she is at risk of failing but she has never started.

She needs to see someone who is fierce and bold, accomplished and tried, true and loyal, and most importantly, someone who has come from a meager background and humble beginnings to prove that she too can overcome what seems to be impossible and unachievable. Values make those accomplishments valuable because I use them to overcome the obstacles and barriers that were supposed to stop me from being successful. She needs to know what is possible and what someone else says about her never being anything is a lie.

My fierceness and focus have to be battle-tested and have proven that values are important to be successful under even the worst of circumstances.

How Does She Do It? Who Does She Think She Is?

Time Management

I am a planner. I have carried around a planner on paper for years. I have spent thousands of dollars on organizational systems so that I can arrive on time and remember everything that I am responsible for. It is what achievers and bosses, leaders and fixers use to be effective.

Time management is key to achievement. When I was in two master degree programs, raising two small children, married then divorced, working full-time, and publishing two to three books each year, which lasted for more than a decade, I only watch three hours of television every week. I can only watch three hours of specific shows on television: Scandal, Gray's anatomy, and Private Practice. all of which happened on Thursday night.

This concept of time management has eluded most people. People are late, they miss meetings, and they are not usually using note taking strategies for the meeting so that they know what happened and what they need to do next.

When you don't know what you have spent your time on, then you can't account for why you have not achieved your goals.

You cannot spend more time watching television and other frivolous things than your goals and still think that you can achieve your goals.

Time management eliminates procrastination. When you plan your time, there is no time for other situations to stop you from getting your work done.

What do you need to change in order to get your time better focused?

Networking

I do not like networking but it is necessary. I do not like shaking hands and kissing babies. I do not like trying to convince people to work with me or to like me or to consider my services and my talents and my skills. Networking is also about getting to know others and to form partnerships so that you can form relationships and collaborations so that more productivity will result.

Networking needs to be focused and streamlined. Ensure that the networks that you form are positive and productive, plausible and powerful.

Networking is the coming together of like-minded persons.

Networking relationships require maintenance. This is a skill that needs practice. It is work, hard work. Building relationships is daily work. It requires that you extend yourself at inconvenient times. I like the outcome of networking, but I do not like the process of networking.

It is sometimes difficult to determine if the result will render the desired outcome.

Keep focused on the outcome.

Follow-Up

The success is in the follow-up. Have you heard that statement before? I did not believe/understand the statement initially - until I used it in order to become a director with Mary Kay, a published author, a motivational speaker, and a franchise owner. And still do three of the four accomplishments.

Make the calls so that you can make the sale and close the deal. Ask the questions. Answer the questions. Figure out the solutions. Chase the leads. Ones you are given and ones you discover.

I attained one of the most elusive feats: Mary Kay Independent Sales Director. I did so in 6 months. This is a position which requires unique discipline and skill set.

Follow up is critical to achieving your goals. You can't just cross your fingers, close your eyes, and hope that it works. You need to make calls, make appointments, send notes, and go to lunches. All so that you can be successful.

Keep organized with phone numbers and email addresses so that you can follow-up with your potential and current clients. I am sure that there's an app for that. Follow-up is an important skill, which you should use because you need to follow-up especially if you are afraid; despite your pride.

Keep asking your clients and leads so that you can reach your goals.

Sometimes it is hard to follow-up but you cannot afford to quit. You cannot afford to lose.

What scares you about the follow-up?

Onedia N. Gage, Ph.D., CLC

HUSTLE

I hustle. I am a hustler. I try and keep trying until I achieve what I am working toward. I do not quit. My hustle is admirable. I impress myself. I impress others - not intentionally, but I do.

If I hustle, then I will not fail. If I consider my achievements and my failures, my dreams and my drive, then I reflect on what I have given to achieve those milestones and elements so that I can count it as a dream come true. I do not consider it a sacrifice; I define it as time management and good decision making. There is no possibility that I will write this book while I am actually watching television. I cannot give up. I cannot quit. I cannot deplete my resources. I cannot lose. I cannot be defeated.

HUSTLE.

I have been unemployed.

I have been homeless.

I have been accused of lying.

I have been accused of cheating.

I have been accused of failing.

I have been accused of inappropriate behavior.

I have been accused of being nonchalant.

I have been accused of being intimidating.

I have been accused of being haughty.

I have been accused of being arrogant.

I have been accused of being infectious.

I have been accused of being charismatic.

But I have never been accused of being lazy or shiftless, lifeless or uninspiring. For that, I am grateful. I am immensely, overwhelmingly excited that others recognize my hustle. and the result of that HUSTLE.

HUSTLE.

ACHIEVE.

HUSTLE.

REST.

REPEAT.

My life has been built around my hustle and my exceptional work ethic. I could always be counted on for that work ethic. I am all that I have. I am the only person that I can count on. EVERY person that I'm supposed to be able to count on has failed me or died. I don't have a choice except to succeed. I do not have anyone to catch me if I were to fail and/or fall. I don't have anyone to talk me off of any ledges or out of any dark places.

I ONLY have me.

I am built totally and completely on that hustle. There were some very distinctive people who have contributed to this HUSTLE: my great-grandfather, my great-grandmother, my grandfather, my father, and my step-father.

My great-grandfather taught me how to fish, wash clothes, cook, and to drive. He also taught me how the grocery shop. He taught me to dream, save and to be uncommon.

We talked as much as you can with a three-year old until I was a young adult. He listened. I talked. He talked. I learned. I listened. He taught me to drive a tractor, pick pecans, and catch crawfish in the puddle behind his garage.

He did it all. My great-grandmother was in a wheelchair because of her heart and whatever else ailed her. I knew that she had a pacemaker but I never asked because I spent my time hoping that when I'm married that if I was in the type of health that my grandmother was in, that I would have the same amazing man that my grandfather was to her. He did it all: yard work, repairs, meals, laundry, healthcare and above all, love. His hustle was more than admirable. I learned how to do it all because that was the standard. I learned how to administer her medication because I could read at 3 years old. I hope that I encouraged him like he inspired me.

Then there was my great-grandmother. She was my matriarch and protector. She held everyone accountable. She was very direct. When she became ill, she did not want me to see her in the hospital. Imagine the position which that put my grandfather and Dad in. I insisted that I was present. When she passed away, my parents weren't speaking to each other. My father did not call or my mother ignored his calls. Either way, I learned of her death because of the obituaries which were posted in the newspaper. The funeral was not pleasant; neither was the wake.

I let the grown-ups know where they had all gone awry. As a 12-year-old, I sat on the side of my great-grandfather and held his hand while he was watching his heartbeat of six decades laid to rest. I dabbed his tears. I did not let anyone talk to us. NOBODY.

She was my strong tower. She reinforced my educational standards. She made sure that I knew what love was. She encouraged me to dream. She is looking down from heaven as proud as a peacock. She knows her contribution to my life - my hustle - knowing that she had done her job.

My father was a networking, multifaceted hustler. music producer. Truck driver. Charismatic. All of that but he could never capitalize on his talents. I do not know if it was money or opportunity or support. I have no idea why he didn't ever become the famous producer he desired to be. In the meantime, in his faults and failures, I learned that relationships are the key to success. I am not great at building those types of relationships. He once dated a lady who owned a jewelry store. I believe that he did it so when my birthday came around, he would have a gift to give me. He had a way with getting his way.

I remember the time that I was standing next to the group who sang 'Let's Just Kiss and Say Goodbye.' In the picture, I am standing near the performers and looking curious. I have no idea why I was standing so close. Surely, my parents should have pulled me closer to them. At any rate, my dad knew a lot of people. It is always interesting to hear 'you are Sam's daughter, right?'

My paternal grandfather had a ranch. We didn't see each other much. He was an entrepreneur but I never knew how he made money from a ranch. I imagine that it is hard to do. Although we did not communicate much, I believe his work ethic affected me as well.

My maternal grandfather worked all day. daily. He would leave home at 5:30 a.m. He arrived home at 9:00 p.m. He operated a crane. He was a longshoreman. I think that it means that he walked the ship. He had a great work reputation. He was always clean. He rewarded me for my grades: $5 for every A and $4 for every B.

He supported my desire to work. My mother was complaining about the distance from our house to the job. My grandfather told her that I would not be quitting, rather he asked her if she needed gas money. In his eyes, earning my own money was the lesson. He could have given me the money that I was earning. It was important to see me build work capacity. He told her to let him know when she needed money, but there would be no more complaints and quitting was not an option.

 I would wake early on Saturdays when I visited my grandparent's home so that I could talk to him. I had questions and wonderings. I wanted to share my dreams with him. I wanted to know what he thought and what could he help me to achieve. He had wit and wisdom that I needed. He is responsible for the number of restaurants where I have eaten because on each birthday, the birthday person was able to select the restaurant of their choice. There was not a limit or boundary. We have been to some of the fanciest places one can imagine.

He worked so much. One day, I asked him why. He said so that he could eat steak whenever he wanted to. He went on to explain that he had grown up on a farm where he had worked really hard as a teenager. He did not want to do that again. His memories of his grandmother were profound. Grandma Sally was a real badass. She was a boss. Although I never actually met her and we only spoke of her a few times, he had a picture of her on his dresser and she made him the man he was. He wanted to make her proud. He only knows how to do that through work. He was proud of himself for taking care of his family - all of us; especially during financial challenges due to the lack of someone like him in every home.

He appreciated my work ethic and told me so. He would be one of my biggest supporter if he were alive now.

My stepfather and I started quite terribly. He was a smoker which I despised. Eventually we worked through that. He could not figure out why I kept changing jobs. He only had three jobs his entire life. But then I reminded him that times had changed and as long as I kept a job, he should not worry. I have worked at different companies for different reasons. I worked at one company so that I could furnish my home with a discount. I worked at some places because I wanted the experience. Overall, he then learned to respect my work ethics so my hustle means something to him. He assumed that I changed jobs more often than he would have because I didn't have a work ethic. Once I proved him otherwise, he changed his point of view. He learned to appreciate my vast experience. He then understood my logic and thought processes.

Because of all of them, hustle is important. I have it, seen it, and exercised it and coach it and teach it and expect it.

Hustle.

Achieve.

Hustle.

Relax.

Repeat.

Coaching

I am always helping others to achieve their dreams and to achieve their goals. I offer advice fluently and without reserve. The problem is that some people do not immediately take action. I'm working on letting that go.

Coaching means so much to me because I wish that I had a me throughout my life. I need people to take life and advice seriously.

As we progress through life, we mature to understand that life is shorter than planned. We need to maximize each day. Nothing is promised. Procrastination is not a good practice. Procrastination is assuming that tomorrow is promised, when it is not.

I have been asked several times when is enough achievement enough. As long as I am gifted, then I am purposed to produce.

Coaching allows me to share what I have been gifted with so that others are blessed. Coaching is helpful to others because the world is stingy. The world does not want others to be great, even when there is more than enough to go around. Stop being stingy. Share. Be fair. Be equitable. Helping others frees me. If you help enough of other people, then you will be blessed and you will get what you want.

GRIT

Grit. Grit is what makes you not quit, to dig into what matters to achieve your goal, and to stick to the plan. Remaining focused is what makes grit possible. I should have quit several times during my life because of many reasons.

Grit is the difference-maker between those who do amazing things and those who quit right before a breakthrough. Success requires failure. Nobody becomes a millionaire or a billionaire without some failures. That failure was not permanent. Grit transforms that temporary setback into something brilliant.

Grit is discovered, developed and encouraged. I had many discoverers of my grit. Mrs. Douglas was one of the first. She ensured that I did not become discouraged. She helped me to facilitate my gifts so that others would not fall apart around me. I needed some wisdom and polish. She spent time making sure how to help people to manage me. She led me. She saw me. I have been looking for her since then - a current version of course. She passed away and I still miss her. And need her. Being able to see the grit in others is what I do now. I do this in others, especially in young people.

My elementary teachers help me to develop that grit. They helped me through understanding my intellectual gifts and supporting me through my personal family crises. My parents got divorced. We were from a small neighborhood and not wealthy. We may have been from the poorest school district which eventually closed because of the poor financial management and theft, but my teachers cared and are memorable. They were invested in me and recognized I had quite a future. I am sure that I am making them proud.

STICKTOITTIVENESS.

Stick-to-it-tiveness is the ability to stay the course, not quit, and definitely not look back. Yes, I made up a word so that I can prove my validation of that word and all that it represents. I stick to what I start. I get discouraged too, but I can't stop or quit. I am on assignment. Some of those assignments are a surprise to me.

Grit also ensures you are successful even when your legacy or family would suggest otherwise. Your background may not be of success but grit makes you change those odds.

Grit overcomes family doubts and discouragement. Your biggest critics and naysayers and the askers of the wrong questions are those closest to you. They really just lack vision and they are not futuristic. They might not actually mean any harm, but the fact is that you will be on an island of achievement if you don't have that in your legacy.

My children have grit. I have taught them through my behavior how to persevere through the events and situations which were designed to make you quit and fail. Grit keeps you going. Grit requires that you find another solution for what seems to be an impossible feat. Grit is understanding that you are on the edge of a breakthrough while you feel like you are about to break down. Grit is when others insist that you quit, but you know that you can't.

Grit is uncomfortable. Grit is not measurable. It is what you cannot see like hair color or eyes. Grit shows up in the results. Grit has fears but ignores them.

Grit is the inner strength that pieces together the fear and the doubt, the obstacles and the bleakness of the possibilities. And still keeps working.

Git is not seen by everyone. some people will never see grit. Even though you have never seen it, it does not mean that you cannot have it.

I hope that you develop grit. I hope that grit develops you.

Achievements

I have achieved many things - most of which I never planned; definitely unexpected. Some of my achievements are overwhelming. I have been in leadership since I was a child - before I even knew what the word leadership was or what it meant. So, I have been a store manager, a consultant, marketing assistant, sales executive, and educator. Not too big a deal, but then being the youngest board member on a major nonprofit which previous average age was 50 years of age, at the age of 28 did feel great.

In one year, I published a book, changed jobs three times, got married, got pregnant, and started building a home. The next year I finished building that house, had a baby, published another book, and moved career locations. One of my friends asked me how do you top this past 2 years?

I had no idea how people perceived me and my accomplishments.

I only wanted to publish two books. Now, I'm sitting at 78 published books; over 100 ISBNs in circulation, and counting. This, I would have never dreamed. Every now and then, you meet the wrong person who said something interesting: 'do you ever stop to celebrate your books?' I had to stop and consider what he said. So, I held a celebration of the 20th book, and I was super disappointed in the attendance of the event. I have been hesitant to host another one since then.

Celebrating when is important. I will add a few to my calendar every year. You should consider doing the same. As I continued to write, education became a key factor. I returned to school for my MBA because I was not feeling valued in my marriage. I achieved the MBA designation under two years. I started the Masters in Education with just a few months left in the MBA program - so yes, I was in school for two degrees at the same time. I graduated in two consecutive summers. Then, I kept going with education.

I just kept going in part because I recalled my goal sheet. As I started marking off of the list, what I did not realize was the accomplishments that were not on the list - things that I never ever dreamed of. I cannot even imagine what I have done. My daughter says that I do not get excited about it, and that I am way too humble. I did not know that was a 'thing.'

I make this life that I have look easy. That was never my intention. I only found this out because someone said 'surely if you can do it then I can do it.' That statement was not made with the spark and enthusiasm it usually is accompanied by. She said it like it was ridiculous that she was not able to achieve what I had. I cannot believe that we were still at this level in life when we don't understand our gifts.

At any rate, I am aware that my accomplishments make people nervous. I do not understand that at all. I've told at least one of my friends that I do not have to and will not be jealous of anything that anyone has because if I want one, then I will go get it. One of my friends has her doctorate in education. So I went and got a doctoral degree. I have some specific plans for that degree.

I taught math class and spent some time helping others to achieve what is requested and what is required.

Achievements are self-esteem enhancers. They will certainly change how you view yourself, as well as how others view you. People are in awe of me. I am not.

Accomplishments and achievements are designed to help others to do the same.

Never 'We Made It'

I will never use the words 'I made it' in reference to what I have done and achieved at all. Definitely not a bragger, so this is outside my behavior and my character.

This is the reason why I can't celebrate too much. That is the start of the fall to me. That is when it is no longer about the work, the intent, or the purpose. It becomes self-centered. We don't get to rub our success in the face of others.

You have the right to celebrate but we operate in a classy manner at all times and we will function in excellence. My success is not the time to make someone feel inferior or less than. I do not apologize, but I do not flaunt.

Being haughty is not a healthy characteristic. It is not healthy to hurt others because of your success. Additionally, I have more to do so I do not have the energy to spend time on anything other than my to-do list; being small is not one of them.

I appreciate my success and I never want it to subside. There will be low moments when I am not successful. I would want grace for those times. I try to treat people the same way I would like to be treated. We have not arrived.

This follows with I do not brag. I do not flaunt. I do not put others down. I do not taunt others when they are not doing their job and I do not mock others. Success is a gift that appears to be the hope for others. Others need to see me in order to start their assignments. You may need that for you to stop procrastinating.

Humble and meek ensures that success lasts longer. Others then will admire your success and your attitude about that success.

How Does She Do It

There was a movie titled 'I don't know how she does it.' Quite funny. But reality to those of us who achieve - especially, specifically me. I am a planner and because of that I have become a logistical guru. I know that pursuing your wildest dreams and goals requires courage - more than some of us can muster. I understand that.

When I first decided to publish the poems that I had been writing since I was 12 years old, I researched to find an agent and a publishing house. I found no one.

I started writing the novel that I always wanted to write. I sent thirty query letters in order to attract the publisher. No one stepped forward to publish me. I could have quit. I could have given up. And almost did.

I was at a friend's house reading his newspaper while I was waiting on him to get ready and I ran across this ad about self-publishing for authors. I studied the company and decided to use them to publish the poetry book. I was pleased so I published the novel as well. That worked for a while until I decided to go in a different direction.

There are a few words which are used to describe me: resourceful, logical, logistically savvy, methodical, and energetic. Perseverance and diligence are also words which describe me.

So, when I am asked how do you balance your life's demands and your personal desires, I have one answer: I do what is important first. I do what is special. I do what has a lasting meaning. I manage my time in such a manner that I will feel accomplished at the end of the day.

That also means I say no. The word no is valuable in achievement. A gentleman said in my presence: no has to be a complete sentence. No has to be used in a complete sentence and that is the end of the conversation.

I do not watch much television. So no, I do not binge watch shows every weekend. As a reward for time spent, I watch a couple of shows. Consider what you could do for your business or family or self if you use that time that is required for you to spend binge watching that show: a season is 20 shows, so 20 hours.

What can you achieve in 20 hours? Your to-do list will be complete. You make a decision about your future when you squander 20 hours and often more by intentionally watching a television series which has already made its money and is now on residual income. You are watching their work in the fruits of their labor, while avoiding your work and toil. Does that seem like the best use of your time? Should you be working instead of watching?

Patience: another quality that assists with achievement. I also say no to spending time with people who I don't actually care for or don't care for me. Understanding the difference between who is in your corner and who supports you versus who is in your business is essential. Once you understand that, then you need to take action. Everyone is not a part of every facet of your life. All people that you know do not make it through every stage in your life, growth, and development.

I do not have a large friend circle. I spend a lot of time alone, because I choose to do that. I could spend time, lots of disingenuine time with people so that I can say that I did that, but what is that worth? It is not important to me to do that. I only want genuine environments. Those are limited and rare. So choose wisely. Be true to yourself, which includes getting to know who that really is - not what others want and expect you to be.

In 2021, I traveled over 20,000 air miles, 15,000 which were alone. I had places that I wanted to go. I decided not to wait on anyone to go with me. I went alone and had an amazing time. I would do it again. I still do.

I enjoyed myself when I am where I chose to go. I am in that moment. If you cannot afford to be present at the moment, then do not go. Be honest with yourself and the host or honoree of the event about your decision. If you're not able to engage at a birthday party for example, without tapping your foot in anxiety because you are thinking about what you NEED to do instead or you are checking your watch often, then handle your business first, which may cause you to miss the event(s).

This also means that you may need to plan better. You need to take a larger view of your calendar so that you can plan so that you don't miss anything and you will have the opportunity to choose where you can attend socially and for networking purposes.

I am not always perfect and on point but I also do not make excuses and I do not let myself off of the hook.

I do it with my entire being.

I am all in.

No brakes.

No breaks.

Read that again.

No brakes.

No breaks.

People will not help or support you if you are fickle or indecisive.

With Two Kids

With two kids. And no husband/boyfriend! I have two children who are now adults at the time of this writing. My children always come first. When I gave birth to my daughter, I stopped doing some extracurricular activities. When my son arrived, I stopped doing additional events. When I pursued my Master's degrees, I did my homework after they were asleep. Yes, I was a little sleep deprived but it was necessary and worth it. I did not want their daytime hours spent with me saying mommy is busy and not now I am working. Kids do not need to be victims of our goals, although they will be the beneficiary of that work.

So, I earned three degrees during their childhood and they witnessed me graduate so they understood the concept of hard work and work ethic.

My two children are also athletes. They have been to football and basketball practices, games, and tournaments. If I could add up the miles that I have traveled, the minutes that I have spent, and the money that I have spent, then I would have a healthy savings or be debt free. What that time, travel, and money represents is the commitment I have to being a mom and ensuring that they are whole human beings. Being fully present and fully invested translates into love. Children define love as time. It means something to them when I show up. And cheer. And motivate. And serve lunch to the team. And hand them water as they entered the bus because the team's managers left the water bottles at the school. And raising money. And creating snack bags on the tournament road trip.

With two kids, I kept my stride and goals. My kids have seen struggle and victory. They have been in the room and at the table when I am making deals. I am committed to raising them. I am a mom first - that is my only job. Mommy is all that I am required to do. Everything else is optional and does not define me. My success is defined and cemented in how they look at me and how they respect me, and how they feel about me and what they say about me to their friends and mates.

I want to lead and inspire them. I want to compel them. I want them to remain humble, while unique. I want them to be comfortable in their own bodies and skins. They need to be able to look at themselves in the mirror and be able to face themselves. I want them to be proud of themselves. I have taught them to depend on and to love each other.

They have filled my life and all that I have done.

I was at work on a Saturday as the store manager - 'living the dream.' The store's phone rang and I answered it as I was closest to it. Her dad said she has taken 18 steps. I wept immediately. I ran back to my office, grabbed my bag, and went home. I had missed her first steps - so unacceptable.

I promise that for the next child it would not happen and it did not. When he walked, I was there, working from home, and I was elated! I want my kids to be prepared for life because I do not want anyone to ask my children 'didn't your mother teach you anything.'

There was the one time when I questioned my priorities because they were in distress. These two kids are my heartbeats.

I love them.

I would not change a moment.

Who Does She Think She Is

Whew! If I had a dollar for every time that this comment was said and thought about me, I would be considerably wealthy!

Be careful when you ask someone that question. You do not know what they will say. What if she says nobody or a bitch? Are you prepared for the answer? No, not actually. Be careful with this question. It speaks of jealousy and disdain. The question then becomes why do you feel that way toward a successful, ambitious woman who is single and just wants to live and not just survive.

Be careful with this approach because if she is an overcomer and a bootstrapper, these are issues that you don't want.

Now, to answer the question: she actually does not think much of herself. I know that I did not. I chose achievement because being a statistic was not an option. I knew that I had to graduate both high school and college because I did not want to be a statistic. I put myself through college. I borrowed money and worked. Life For Me Ain't Been No Crystal Stair by Langston Hughes. My family just did not have the financial means and the ability to teach.

I learned by looking. I learned by attaching myself to people who are respected and who mentored me. I am sure that I'm not the only one who struggled to be together in their life. But when you make the most of it, then you will be questioned, criticized, and shamed.

It does not matter what you say. I am here on this Earth to make a difference and to fulfill a purpose. At some point, you may want to stop focusing on me and what I am doing to figure out yourself and your priorities.

Does it really matter who I think I am? Does it really matter what have I achieved? How does that stop you from doing what you were supposed to be and are designed to do?

Do not make the mistake of focusing on me and others like me and by doing so, you miss out on your own calling. This is the mistake most people realize. While you were spending time on someone else and what they are doing, you should be doing your own thing.

So, who is she?

She is a seeker of goodness and achievement. She is an amazing human being. She is an awesome person. She keeps focus on her purpose. She is a giver. She is a trooper. She is an overcomer. She believes. She is an overachiever. She is a creator. She believes. She is a powerful being. She is a doer. She is a visionary. She is an organizer. She is a thinker. She is reflective. She is smart. She has given herself permission to do everything that she desires. This permission is huge.

Our grandmothers and mothers only did what was socially, culturally, and academically acceptable. there was an understanding of what women could and could not do before 1970. As of 1971, those rules changed.

She does not need anyone's permission in order to be the woman that she is called to be.

That she is me.

I do not need and will not request your permission to be smart, wealthy, kind, and productive. I do not need your consignment on what I want to achieve. I am totally able to pursue my dreams, desires, goals, and purpose, without checking to see if my movements will wilt your fragile self-esteem.

'Who does she think she is' is inappropriate for you to ask or think or suggest.

She may not know who she is but let her do whatever she is doing with peace, without ridicule, without criticism, without doubt, and without barriers, roadblocks, and obstacles named after you.

She spent time developing, researching, and creating this work. It has been her dream for a long time. She is deserving because she put her hand to the plow.

If you cannot support her authentically and be proud that she is someone that you know personally, then do not just add to her stress with your jealousy.

Who does she think she is. . .?

She is more powerful than she knows.

She is more resourceful than she realizes.

She is more creative than she dreamed.

She is more caring than we deserve.

She is a thinker.

She is a dreamer.

She is loving.

She is a seeker.

She is not concerned about the rest of the world.

She is not easily distracted.

She is a risk taker.

She is determined.

She is charismatic.

She is a decision maker.

She is decisive.

She is an overcomer.

She is loyal.

She is dedicated.

She is a hard worker.

She is a game changer.

She has grit.

She is more than this list can mention.

That is who she is - not who she thinks she is. Most of the time when people ask that question, the intent is unfortunate. It is based on jealousy and sometimes malice. The question is mentioned with disgust and disdain. Stop asking this question.

Start asking the best questions:

1. How can I start to pursue my dreams based on what she has inspired me to pursue and achieve?

2. How can I stop procrastinating so that I can achieve what I had My Mind Set On?

3. What does the success that I desire require?

4. When will I pursue it?

5. When will I stop being concerned about what others will think, do, or say when I pursue my dreams and goals?

6. How can I support someone who is brave enough to avoid the outside noise and to pursue what others do not have the courage to pursue?

These are the questions and concerns that we should be pursuing because she deserves our encouragement rather than our doubt. don't be a part of the world's naysayers.

By the way, she is not worried about being better than you. She is concerned about being better than she ever imagined. She does not need your permission or consent. When she got the courage to get started, you never actually crossed her mind.

Onedia N. Gage, Ph.D., CLC

What Has She Achieved?
What is It Worth to Her?

I have achieved some accolades that I never envisioned that I would. I cannot have imagined that I would have earned four degrees. I have created my own publishing company. I have an international distribution for my books that are available worldwide. I have over 100 ISBNs in circulation between printed materials and ebooks. I've been a successful classroom teacher, an instructional coach, assistant principal, and mentor. I am a certified life coach. I've been an amazing motivational speaker. I have over 100 videos on my YouTube channels.

I have raised two amazing children who are equipped to take over the world, because they are equipped to do so. They are both athletes. They are both intelligent. They are both entrepreneurs. They are well mannered and respectful. They have a vision for the future. They are also dreamers. I own a consulting and coaching business. I have over 50 clients. I do individual and group coaching sessions.

I have two radio talk shows. We have covered a wide range of topics from Health and Wellness to marriage and family. I've opened two national franchises and I'm working on a third location. I work very hard in order to enjoy the lifestyle that I want to live. there are aspects of my life which I have never dreamed of doing.

I need to achieve my dreams because I have worked hard to do so.

I have a list of goals that is 49 lines and two pages long; so roughly 100 items on the list. I work every day to achieve something on that list.

As I pursue my purpose, my calling, my dreams, my goals, and my life's work, I do not consider the thoughts and feelings of others. I am pursuing what I want because it is what I need to be satisfied. I worked hard in order to reach my wildest dreams.

My work means everything to me. It only comes second to my children. My work requires a lot of time, but it is time well spent. I do not want to fail. I also want to leave a legacy for my children. I want them to inherit something more than heartache and bills.

I want them to be proud of me and the legacy that we generate. I want them to look back over their lives and realize that they are blessed because of their legacy and their life.

There are some things that I want to achieve so that I can say that I can and did. I want to do it because the odds are against me.

I get excited when I reach my goals. I really work hard to make my goals a reality. I will persist until I reach my goals and dreams.

Lastly, it is important to me and brings me great joy when I see how proud my children are of me.

We are making this legacy up from scratch one day at a time.

Work-Life Balance

Another contributor to my success is work-life balance. I have managed to live a balanced life. I take the time to relax. I spend time prioritizing my life and the work that I have. I need to ensure that I'm able to relax and work in proportion.

I want to have a great work ethic but I don't want to work myself into an unhealthy situation. I want to have fun and travel, eat well and enjoy my children.

Work-life balance is doable and attainable. This is the most important part of success - balance. This is a fast world and in order to keep up, there are details and elements which are sometimes neglected. Sleep is one of them. I try to rest at least 6 hours each night. I wake up late on weekend mornings. I travel so that I can rejuvenate my body, mind, and soul. I have regular hair, nails, feet and waxing appointments. I get massages regularly. I regulate my self-care so that I have something to look forward to. I like to be able to schedule my appointments after my most stressful work so that I can look forward to my time to relax. My life is not as stressful as it could be but I still need to maintain balance.

I do not easily overwhelm or have anxiety either so I can take on whatever projects that I see fit for me and my family.

I do not party or go to clubs. I am home by 10:00 p.m. on most nights. I live a safe life.

This is critical for a good life.

It is hard to be successful and not enjoy the fruits of that labor.

Onedia N. Gage, Ph.D., CLC

Advice

After all of these pages, I believe that you have enough to be successful in your life and with pursuing your goals.

If I was giving advice, then the following is my advice:

1. Stay focused.

2. Write your goals down with dates.

3. Share your goals with important people.

4. Schedule your regular self-care.

5. Persevere.

6. Be determined.

7. Keep your priorities at the top of the list of what you focus on.

8. Don't quit.

9. Plan your work.

10. Develop Grit.

This is quite the section but it will remain short. I've given so much information on these pages, this short list is comprehensive enough to assist you with achieving your goals.

The Secret of My Success–Conclusion

My Success is the result of late nights, early mornings, weekends at home, time sacrifices, and a consistent work cadence. None of this happens overnight. You are just experiencing the result of what you do not see. I do not spend my time frivolously. I have to be serious about my results.

The secret is the hard work which is required for that success. There aren't any shortcuts. I have strict requirements about what I spend my time on and who I spend my time with. Do what you actually love, not what you are good at but extremely hate. Do not follow the path someone else has chartered for you. Be aware of your personal mantra. Do what drives you, what keeps you awake at night, and whatever stays on your mind. Pursue what you love with all of your mind, your heart, and your being.

I want the best for you. Stay focused on yourself and make decisions to move forward with your goals, dreams, and life's pursuits.

Let me encourage you to get out of your own way so that you can look at yourself in the mirror again and be proud of yourself as being. You can't be mad at yourself for not achieving and then still not try to achieve.

Please take the opportunity to stop avoiding what could be the greatest thing you have ever done because of fear and a hundred other reasons for not moving forward.

Do it big!

Do it afraid!

Do it now!

If you decide to fail then make sure it is because you tried something, not because you did nothing.

Go for it.

Success is fun!

Fear and avoidance are draining and stifling.

What if I succeed?

I am going to produce!

Welcome to the success center.

Resources

Coachonedia.com

Onediagagespeaks.com

What Did You Say? Affirmations. Encouragement. Motivation.
By Onedia N. Gage

In 90 Days: What Will You Do? By Onedia N. Gage

The Best 40 Days of My Life By Onedia N. Gage

Reflections

_____

_____

_____

_____

_____

_____

_____

_____

_____

_____

_____

_____

_____

_____

_____

_____

_____

_____

_____

_____

_____

Reflections

_____

_____

_____

_____

_____

_____

_____

_____

_____

_____

_____

_____

_____

_____

_____

_____

_____

_____

_____

_____

Reflections

_____

_____

_____

_____

_____

_____

_____

_____

_____

_____

_____

_____

_____

_____

_____

_____

_____

_____

_____

Appendix

Goals

      How to create them

      How to reach them

Mission

Vision

Values

Dreams

Goals

goal [gohl] *noun*

the result or achievement toward <u>which</u> effort is directed; aim; end.

The questions that you answer when developing goals are as follows:

1. What do I want to accomplish?
2. When do I want to accomplish this by?
3. Who is going to help me and hold me accountable?
4. What do you do when you do not meet the goals as planned?
5. Who do you share your successes with?

Goals

Goals	By When	Who

Goals

Goals   **By When**   **Who**

_____

_____

_____

_____

_____

_____

_____

_____

_____

_____

_____

_____

_____

_____

_____

_____

_____

_____

Mission Statement

A personal mission statement is based on habit 2 of <u>7 Habits of Highly Effective People</u> called begin with the end in mind. In one's life, the most effective way to begin with the end in mind is to develop a mission statement one that focuses what you want to be in terms of character and what you want to do in reference to contribution of achievements. Writing a mission statement can be the most important activity an individual can take to truly lead one's life.

Victor Hugo once said there is nothing as powerful as an idea whose time has finally come, you may call it a credo, a philosophy, you may call it a purpose statement, it's not as important as to what you call it, no it's how you define your definition. That mission and vision statement is more powerful more significant, more influential, than the baggage of the past, or even the accumulated noise of the present.

What is a mission statement you ask? Personal mission statements based on correct principles are like a personal constitution, the basis for making major, life-directing decisions, the basis for making daily decisions in the midst of the circumstances and emotions that affect our lives.

Your statement may be a few words or several pages, but it is not a "to do" list. It reflects your uniqueness and must speak to you powerfully about the person you are and the person you are becoming.

Why should you write a personal mission statement?

Numerous experts on leadership and personal development emphasize how vital it is for you to craft your own personal vision for your life. Warren Bennis, Stephen Covey, Peter Senge, and others point out that a powerful vision can help you succeed far beyond where you'd be without one. That vision can propel you and inspire those around you to reach their own dreams.

Q: How do I go about creating my Personal Mission Statement?

A: A Mission Statement is defined as having goals and a deadline. This is opposed to the notion that a Mission Statement is just a bunch of flowery, general phrases like, "I will be the best business person I can be."

What should you include when writing a great personal mission statement?

- describe your best characteristics and how you express them
- have specific, measurable outcomes (or goals)
- have a deadline — for example, December 31st 2012, or a year from today.

When Stephen Covey talks about 'mission statement' in this quote he is referring to the articulation of your life purpose. "If you don't set your goals based upon your Mission Statement, you may be climbing the ladder of success only to realize, when you get to the top, you're on the WRONG BUILDING." **Stephen Covey – 7 Habits of Highly Effective People.**

Mission Statement Example – Poor (It's more like a Vision Statement)

"I aspire to start my own business. I want to help others and be a better businesswoman. I will deliver the best food with the highest service levels." Jane

Mission Statement Example – Better

"I will start my business within 3 months and plan to grow it to $500,000 in revenues within a year. Using this success my staff and I will spread the word to local schools and businesses about eco-friendly food production in order that we reach at least 100 people within the same time frame. My purpose will be to massively add value to our local community in measurable ways that have a real impact on people's health now and in the future" Jane

What to do with your Mission Statement?

So now we have a mission we can set a range of goals on the road to achieving your outcomes and dreams. Your values are clarified and should be in line with the goals you want to achieve in life so you should find it easier to make decisions and to do the "right thing" because you can simply ask yourself, "Will this help me achieve my mission?"

You can even put your mission statement in an area where your family or even co-workers will see it. For, a mission statement defines who you are and what you stand for. This lets people see how you think and feel, which in turn, will help them respect, think and act in line with your values too.

Mission Statement

_____

_____

_____

_____

_____

_____

_____

_____

_____

_____

_____

_____

_____

_____

_____

_____

_____

_____

_____

_____

Vision Statement

A personal vision/mission statement is the framework for creating a powerful life.

Your personal vision statement provides the direction necessary to guide the course of your days and the choices you make about your life.

The idea is to craft a broad-based idea about your life and what will really make it exciting and fulfilling, that's your life vision.

From the vision, you craft a more focused and action orientated "mission" statement based on "purpose". And finally, you get to a list of goals, wishes, desires and needs.

In his book 'The Success Principles', Jack Canfield tells us that in order to create a balanced and successful life; your vision needs to include the following seven areas:

1. work and career
2. finances
3. recreation and free time
4. health and fitness
5. relationships
6. personal goals
7. contribution to the larger community

It does not include the distinctive ways that you intend to accomplish your purpose.

Why Write a Personal Vision Statement?

To express:

- your purpose
- your life's dream
- your core values & beliefs

- what you want for yourself
- what you want to contribute to others
- what you want to be

Characteristics of a Vision Statement:

- Engages your heart & spirit
- Taps into embedded concerns & needs
- Asserts what you want to create
- Is something worth going for
- Provides meaning to the work you do
- Is a little cloudy and grand
- Is simple
- Is a living document
- Provides a starting place from which to get more specificity
- Is based on quality and dedication

Key Elements of a Vision Statement:

- Written down and referred to daily
- Written in present tense, as if it has already been completed
- Includes a variety of activities and time frames
- Filled with descriptive details that anchor it to reality

What Visions Are Not:

- A mission statement: "Why do we exist now?"
- A strategic plan: "How do we plan to get there?"
- A set of objectives: "We will accomplish X by Y time to Z% target audience."

Use these questions to guide your thoughts:

- What are the ten things you most enjoy doing? Be honest. These are the ten things without which your weeks, months, and years would feel incomplete.
- What three things must you do every single day to feel fulfilled in your work?

- What are your five-six most important values?
- Your life has a number of important facets or dimensions, all of which deserve some attention in your personal vision statement.
- Write one important goal for each of them: physical, spiritual, work or career, family, social relationships, financial security, mental improvement and attention, and fun.
- If you never had to work another day in your life, how would you spend your time instead of working?
- When your life is ending, what will you regret not doing, seeing, or achieving?
- What strengths have other people commented on about you and your accomplishments? What strengths do you see in yourself?

Vision Statement

_____

_____

_____

_____

_____

_____

_____

_____

_____

_____

_____

_____

_____

_____

_____

_____

_____

_____

_____

Values Statement

A personal value is absolute or relative and ethical value, the assumption of which can be the basis for ethical action. A *value system* is a set of consistent values and measures. A *principle value* is a foundation upon which other values and measures of integrity are based.

Some values are physiologically determined and are normally considered objective, such as a desire to avoid physical pain or to seek pleasure. Other values are considered subjective, vary across individuals and cultures, and are in many ways aligned with belief and belief systems. Types of values include ethical/moral values, doctrinal/ideological (religious, political) values, social values, and aesthetic values. It is debated whether some values that are not clearly physiologically determined, such as altruism, are intrinsic, and whether some, such as acquisitiveness, should be classified as vices or virtues. Values have been studied in various disciplines: anthropology, behavioral economics, business ethics, corporate governance, moral philosophy, political sciences, social psychology, sociology and theology to name a few.

Values can be defined as broad preference concerning appropriate courses of action or outcomes. As such, values reflect a person's sense of right and wrong or what "ought" to be. "Equal rights for all", "Excellence deserves admiration", and "People should be treated with respect and dignity" are representative of values. Values tend to influence attitudes and behavior.

Values Statement

_____

_____

_____

_____

_____

_____

_____

_____

_____

_____

_____

_____

_____

_____

_____

_____

_____

_____

_____

_____

Dreams

Dreams

_____

_____

_____

_____

_____

_____

_____

_____

_____

_____

_____

_____

_____

_____

_____

_____

_____

_____

_____

_____

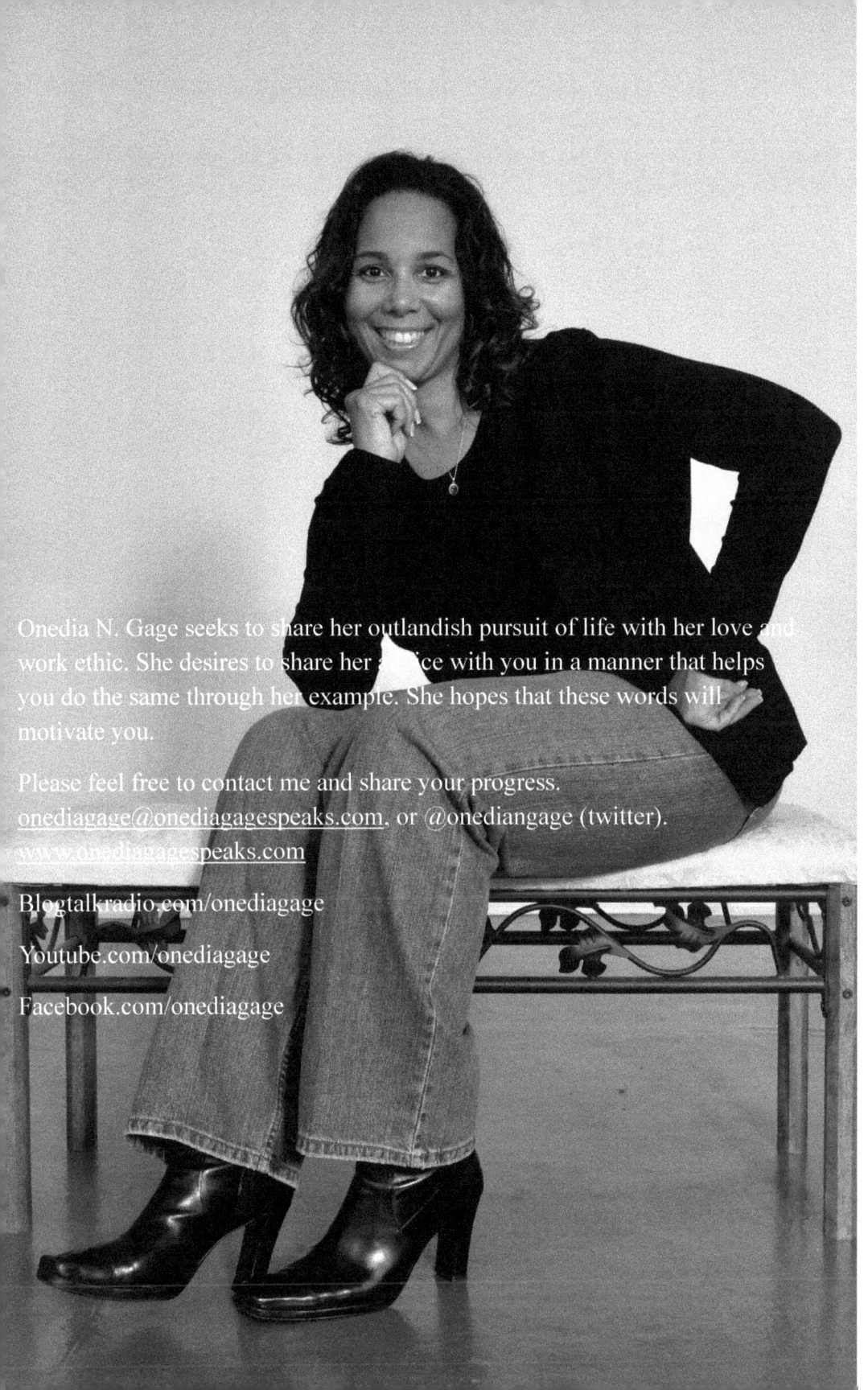

Onedia N. Gage seeks to share her outlandish pursuit of life with her love and work ethic. She desires to share her advice with you in a manner that helps you do the same through her example. She hopes that these words will motivate you.

Please feel free to contact me and share your progress.
onediagage@onediagagespeaks.com, or @onediangage (twitter).
www.onediagagespeaks.com

Blogtalkradio.com/onediagage

Youtube.com/onediagage

Facebook.com/onediagage

COACH ♦ ADVOCATE ♦ TEACHER ♦ FACILITATOR

CONFERENCE SPEAKER ♦ WORKSHOP LEADER

To invite Dr. Gage to speak at your school, business, or organization,

Please contact us at: www.onediagagespeaks.com

@onediangage (twitter) ♦ onediagage@onediagagespeaks.com ♦ facebook.com/onediagage

youtube.com/onediagage ♦ blogtalkradio.com/onediagage ♦ ongage (Instagram)

www.ingramcontent.com/pod-product-compliance
Lightning Source LLC
Chambersburg PA
CBHW040858210326
41597CB00029B/4885